VOCAL SELECTIONS from
HIGH SPIRITS

INCLUDES MATERIAL NOT IN PREVIOUS EDITIONS!

By Hugh Martin and Timothy Gray

ISBN 0-634-02397-7

TRO CROMWELL MUSIC
The RICHMOND ORGANIZATION

EXCLUSIVELY DISTRIBUTED BY

HAL•LEONARD®
CORPORATION
7777 W. BLUEMOUND RD. P.O. BOX 13819 MILWAUKEE, WI 53213

Hugh Martin was born in Birmingham, Alabama and educated at the Birmingham Conservatory of Music. A talented songwriter and accomplished pianist, he was heavily influenced by the music of George Gershwin and contributed many a standard of his own to Broadway and to Hollywood. On Broadway, "Buckle Down, Winsocki," "Ev'ry Time" and "You Are for Loving," were co-written with Ralph Blane for the 1941 *Best Foot Forward*. Solo efforts include the score for *Look, Ma I'm Dancin'* and the musical *Make a Wish* (though some lyrics were contributed by Timothy Gray). Songs for film include: "The Boy Next Door," "The Trolley Song" and "Have Yourself a Merry Little Christmas," all written for *Meet Me in St. Louis* (1944) and "An Occasional Man," written for *The Gold Rush* (1955), again co-authored with Blanc. According to the American Society of Composers, Authors and Publishers, "Have Yourself a Merry Little Christmas" is among the Top 10 most performed songs of all time. His talents as an arranger have been heard on the Broadway stage in *The Boys from Syracuse*, *Gentlemen Prefer Blondes* and *Top Banana*, and in the films *Girl Crazy*, *Broadway Rhythm* and *Presenting Lily Mars*. As pianist, Mr. Martin accompanied Judy Garland during her legendary 1951 Palace Theatre engagement. More recently he can be heard on *Michael Feinstein Sings the Hugh Martin Songbook*, recorded for Nonesuch Records in 1995. *Meet Me in St. Louis* was revived on Broadway in 1990 and several songs were added, including "A Day in New York" as well as "I Happen to Love You" and "Ice," borrowed from his earlier Hallmark Hall of Fame TV Production *Hans Brinker and the Silver Skates*. Mr. Martin was twice nominated for Academy Awards: in 1944 for "The Trolley Song" (*Meet Me in St. Louis*), and in 1947 for "Pass That Peace Pipe" (*Good News*). In 1983 he was inducted into the Songwriters' Hall of Fame.

Timothy Gray has worn many hats over the years. In addition to having written music, lyrics and books for musicals, he has also directed, produced and performed on stage and on television. His credits include: *Love from Judy* (lyrics, co-author of music, staging of musical numbers), *Welcome Darlings* (sketches, lyrics, staging of musical numbers, performer), *From Here and There* (sketches and lyrics), *Airs on a Shoestring* (sketches, lyrics, staging of musical numbers), *Taboo Revue* (sketches, lyrics, producer, director), and *September Song: The Musical World of Kurt Weill* (book and director). He also contributed some lyrics for Hugh Martin's Broadway *Make a Wish*, and produced an Off-Broadway revival of the Kurt Weill-Paul Green *Johnny Johnson*. Yet he still found time to write the book, lyrics and, along with Dennis Buck, the music for *One Wonderful Night* (adapted from Oliver Goldsmith's *She Stoops to Conquer*). Recent projects have included the writing, direction and production of an Off-Broadway show about Judy Garland. As songwriter, Mr. Gray has penned the standards "You'd Better Love Me" and "Meet Me in St. Louis – Louis" as well as countless vocal arrangements, including special material for *Good News* and *Ziegfeld Follies*. For TV he appeared on and often arranged for the "Patrice Munsel Show," "Washington Square" (starring Ray Bolger) and "Revlon Revue" (starring Peggy Lee). A list of artists who have performed or recorded material written by Mr. Gray include Edie Adams, Kaye Ballard, Ray Charles, Petula Clarke, Noël Coward, Ella Fitzgerald, Stan Getz, Tammy Grimes, Jack Jones, Steve Lawrence, Debbie Reynolds, Mel Tormé and Nancy Wilson. Mr. Gray has been seen sporting a new hat recently: he opened an entertainment/music room, "The High Spirits Room," in New York.

Hugh Martin and Timothy Gray first collaborated in 1951 on the London stage production *Love from Judy*. As early as 1953 they wanted to adapt Noël Coward's play *Blithe Spirit*, but permission was not granted until seven years later. Initially titled *Faster than Sound*, *High Spirits* opened at the Alvin Theatre on April 7, 1964.

from the Lester Osterman-Robert Fletcher-Richard Horner production "HIGH SPIRITS"

HOME SWEET HEAVEN

Words and Music by HUGH MARTIN
and TIMOTHY GRAY

sings there,_ Sa-lo-me swings there. In my Home Sweet Heav-en._
Sem-ple_ has built a tem-ple In my Home Sweet Heav-en._

My house is mod-est,_ It's by Ber-ni-ni_ And I've a
There's Doc-tor Crip-pen,_ he's ver-y chum-my_ With Liz-zie

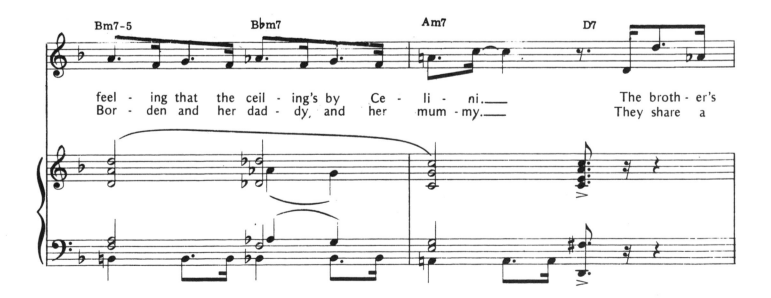

feel — ing that the ceil — ing's by Ce-li-ni._ The broth-er's
Bor-den and her dad-dy, and her mum-my._ They share a

6

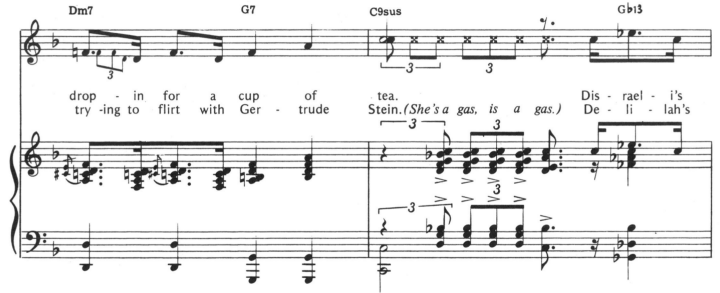

Am7-5   D9   Gm7   A9

fun when Jul - ius Cae - sar___ Proust and St. The - re - sa___
real - ly bowl you o - ver___ Watch - ing Ca - sa - no - va___

Dm7   G7   C9sus   Gb13

drop - in for a cup of tea. Dis - rael - i's
try - ing to flirt with Ger - trude Stein. *(She's a gas, is a gas.)* De - li - lah's

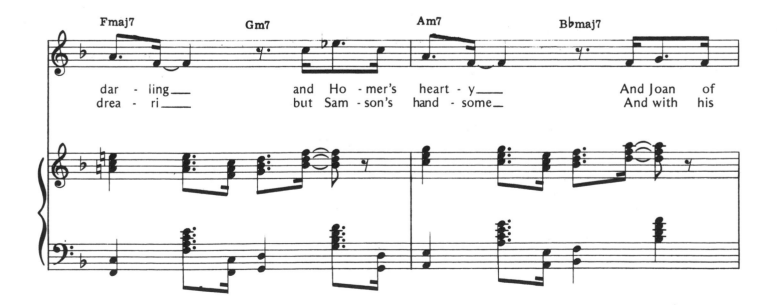

Fmaj7   Gm7   Am7   Bbmaj7

dar - ling___ and Ho - mer's heart - y___ And Joan of
drea - ri___ but Sam - son's hand - some___ And with his

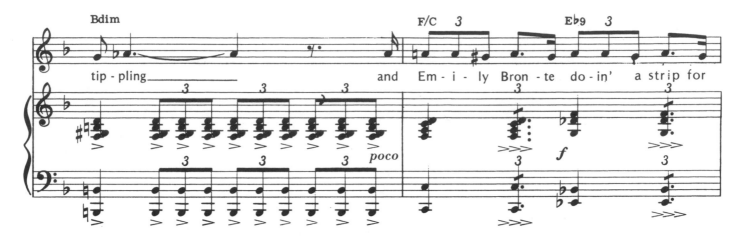

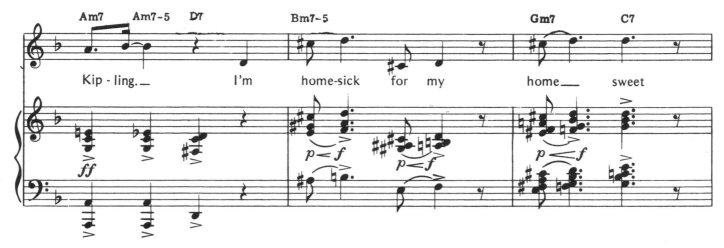

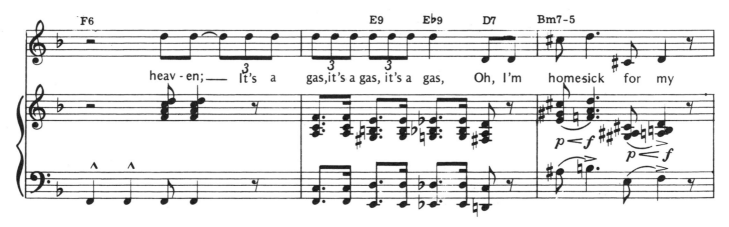

Home Sweet Heaven

Encore Chorus

There's Mussolini
Draped in a sari,
Mad as a hatter, like a fatter Mata Hari.
He splits a kipper
With Jack the Ripper
In my Home Sweet Heaven.
We often dine on
Divine spaghetti
In a little fun place, run by Sacco and Vanzetti
Where I sip vino
With Valentino
In my Home Sweet Heaven.
I miss Tallulah dramatizing,
Judy vocalizing,
(Spoken on pitch) Joan Crawford and her motherly advice.
And when I waltz with Leslie Howard,
Or laugh with Noël Coward,
Then it's really paradise.
Lady Godiva is going steady
With old King Ethelred
Who's hardly ever ready.
They share a chalet
With Walter Raleigh
And his good Queen Bessie,—
It's rather messy.
I miss the concerts by Puccini and Rossini,—
And even that old chicken,—Tetrazzini.
I'm homesick for my Home Sweet 1-2 Heaven,
And it's a gas, it's a gas, it's a gas,
I'm homesick for my Home Sweet Heaven.

from the Lester Osterman-Robert Fletcher-Richard Horner production "HIGH SPIRITS"

WAS SHE PRETTIER THAN I?

Words and Music by HUGH MARTIN
and TIMOTHY GRAY

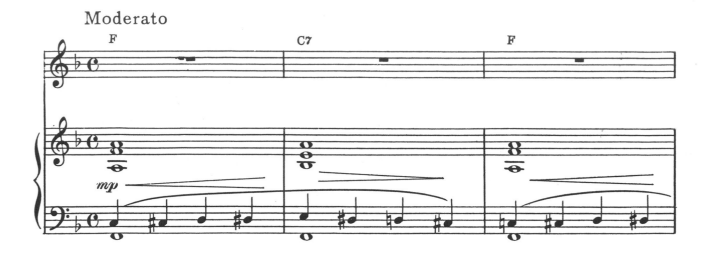

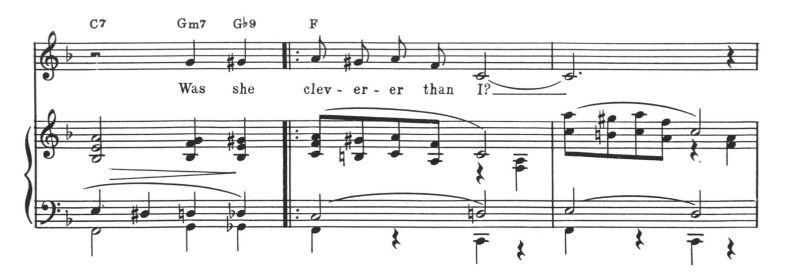

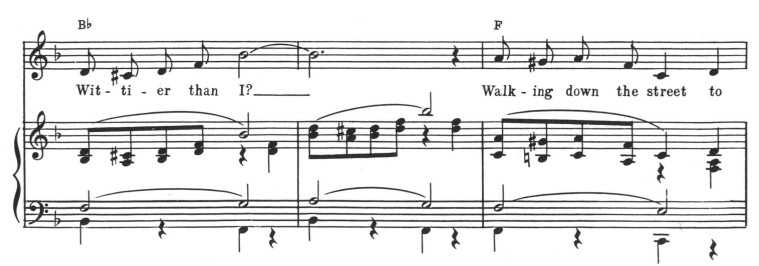

meet you, Was She Pret - ti - er Than I?_____

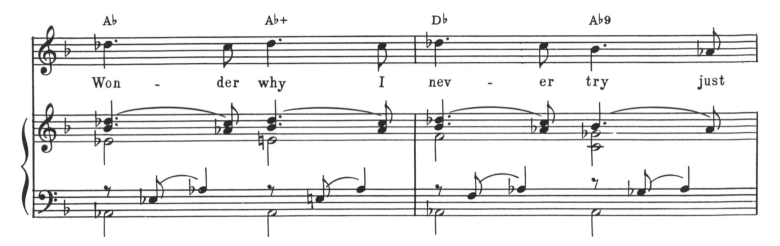

Won - der why I nev - er try just

ask - ing, un - less____ I was too a -

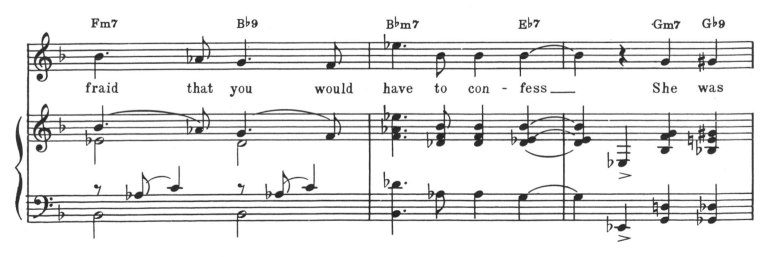

fraid that you would have to con - fess____ She was

clev - er - er than I, _____ Wit - ti - er than I, _____

And I might as well ac - cept it, she was

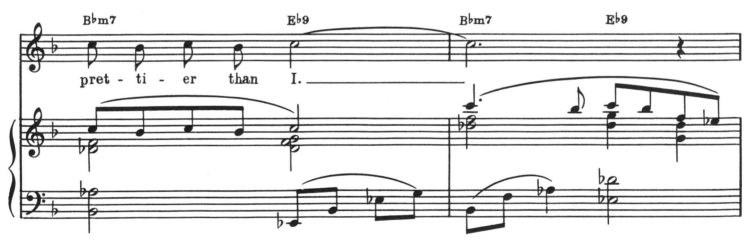

pret - ti - er than I. _____

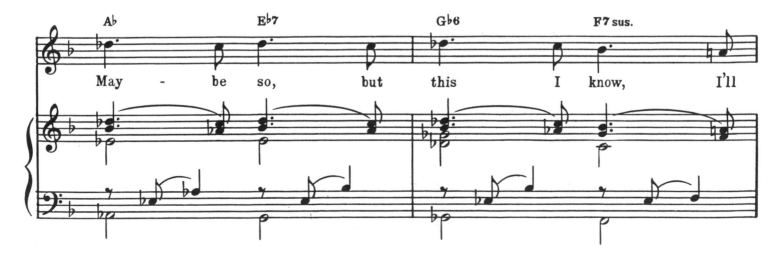

May - be so, but this I know, I'll

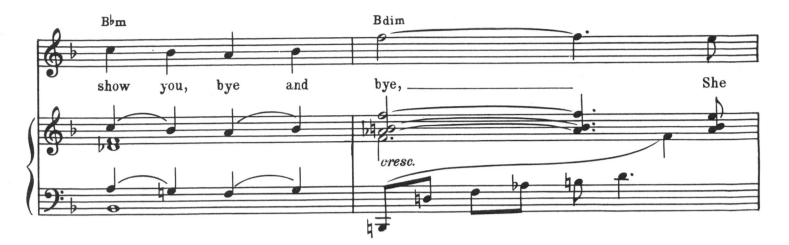

show you, bye and bye, _____ She

nev - er could have loved you _____ half as much as

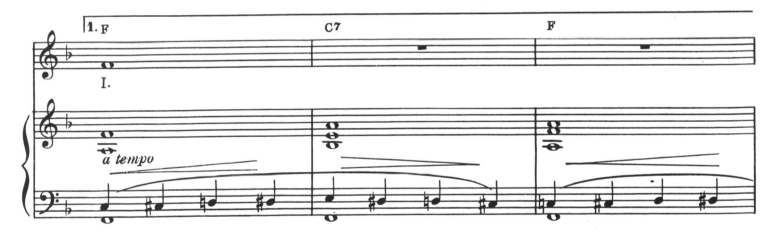

I.

Was she I.

from the Lester Osterman-Robert Fletcher-Richard Horner production "HIGH SPIRITS"

IF I GAVE YOU

Words and Music by HUGH MARTIN
and TIMOTHY GRAY

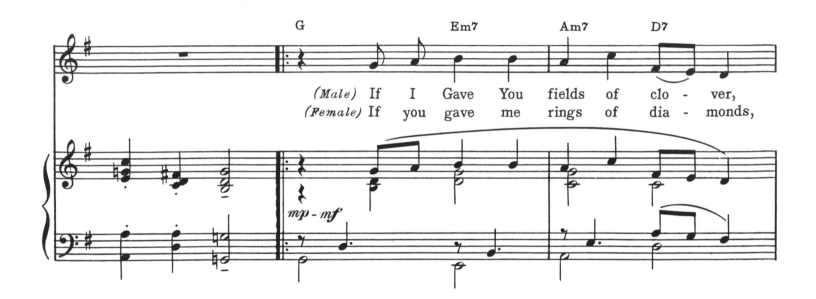

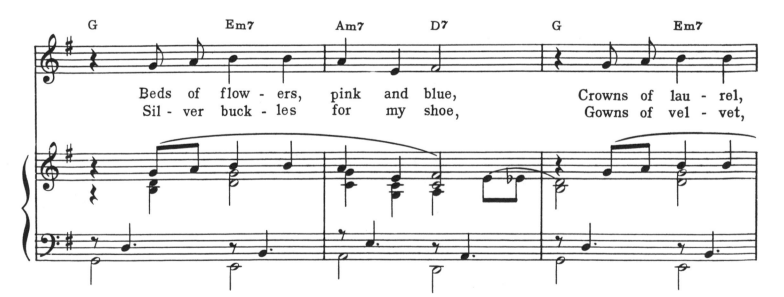

jade,   a clus - ter of pearls,
wine,   a pal - ace of mist,

A show - er of stars ____ for your curls. ____
A brace - let of moons ____ for my wrist. ____

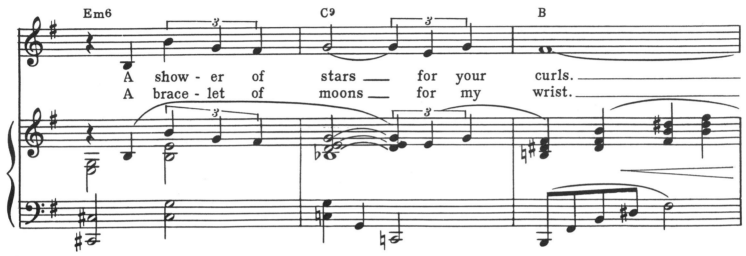

But I have no prides of li - ons,
But I need no rings of dia - monds;

poco rit.   a tempo

And my pearls, a - las, are few.   But for worlds of
One of glass will sure - ly do,   And for worlds of

lov - ing heart - beats, Would you let me stay
lov - ing heart - beats, I will glad - ly stay

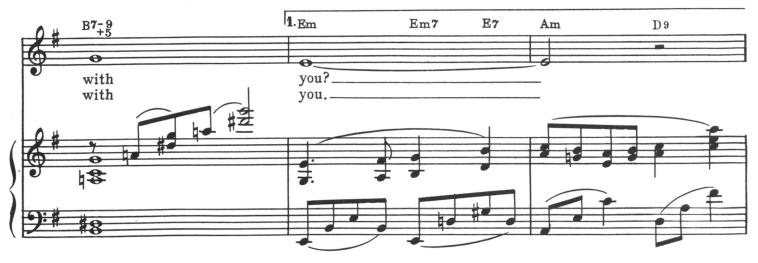

with you?
with you.

you?
you.

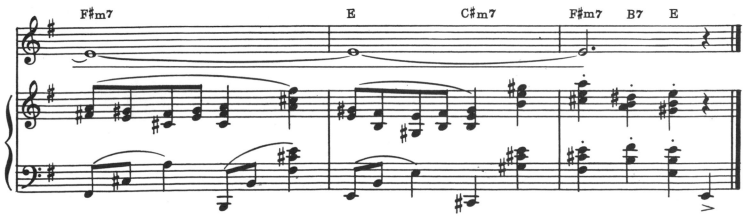

from the Lester Osterman-Robert Fletcher-Richard Horner production "HIGH SPIRITS"

SOMETHING TELLS ME

Words and Music by HUGH MARTIN
and TIMOTHY GRAY

Bright show tempo

Pop lyric: Some-thing Tells Me to-night is the
Show lyric: Some-thing Tells Me to-night is the

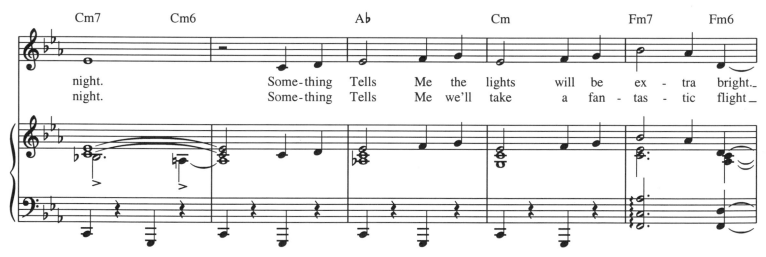

night.   Some-thing Tells Me the lights will be ex- tra bright._
night.   Some-thing Tells Me we'll take a fan- tas- tic flight _

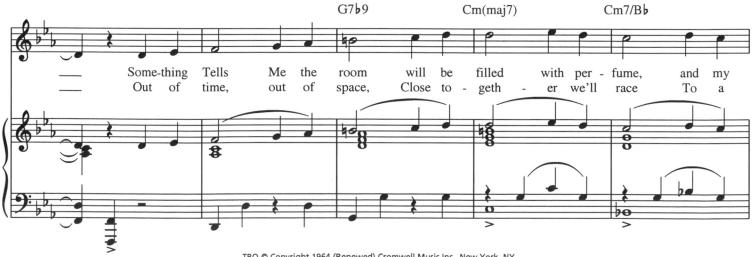

_ Some-thing Tells Me the room will be filled with per- fume, and my
_ Out of time, out of space, Close to- geth- er we'll race To a

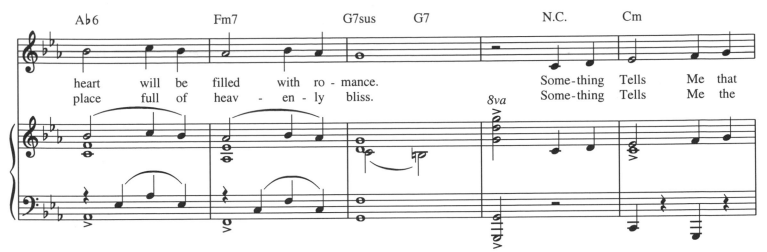

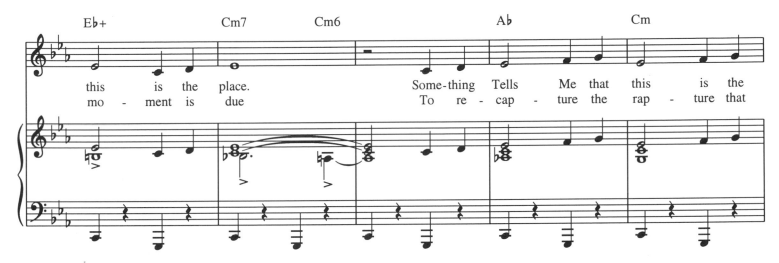

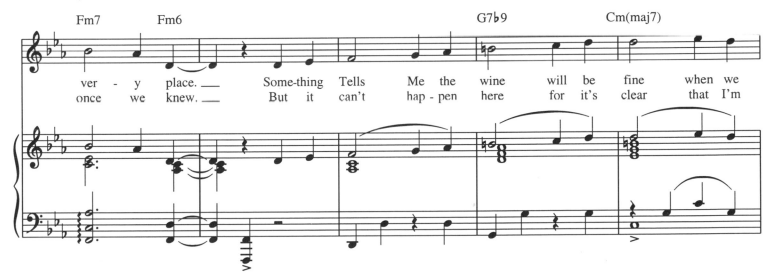

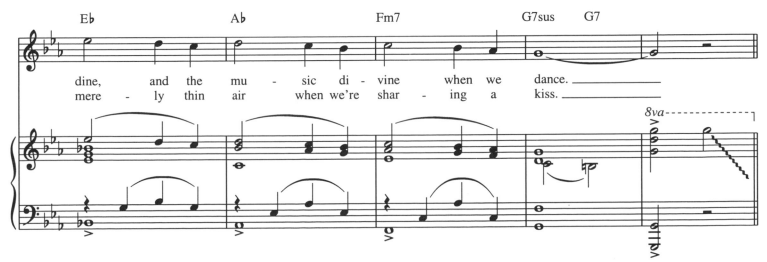

A la romantic Tango (*l'istesso tempo*)

Strange as it seems, stars ap - pear to be show - er - ing down. ____
Spin with me now, spin a - way from the clam - or - ing crowd ____

____ And, as in all of my dreams, we're on top of this
____ Come and be - gin with me now this ad - ven - ture that

Tempo I

shim - mer - ing town. ____ With {your/my} wind - swept face, and {your/my}
fate has al - lowed ____ We'll be high a - bove in the

up - swept hair, and {your/my} fa - vor - ite down - swept gown. Some - thing
sky a - bove on my fa - vor - ite star - crossed cloud. Some - thing

from the Lester Osterman-Robert Fletcher-Richard Horner production "HIGH SPIRITS"

FOREVER AND A DAY

Words and Music by HUGH MARTIN
and TIMOTHY GRAY

for I can share them with you. — Time will go se-rene-ly on and

on, as, hand in hand, we go from dawn to dawn.

Chorus - Smoothly with feeling

The leaves will float on the breeze; the breeze will float on the seas, For-

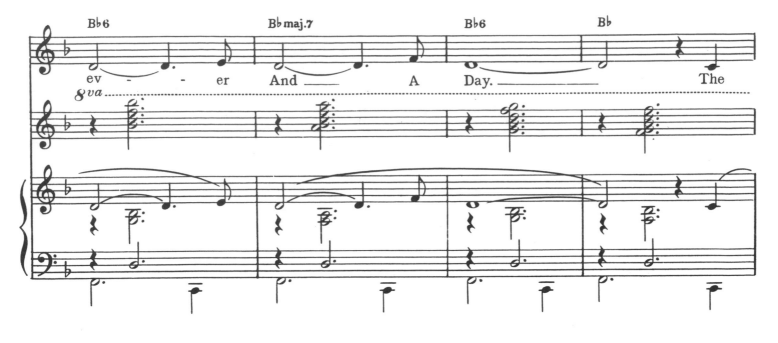

Guar - dian an - gels will sing to me,____ Ev - 'ry
*Fall will al - ways be spring to me,____ When you

time that you cling to me. And you'll see the love we'll give through the years will
ten - der - ly cling to me.

molto rit. *a tempo*

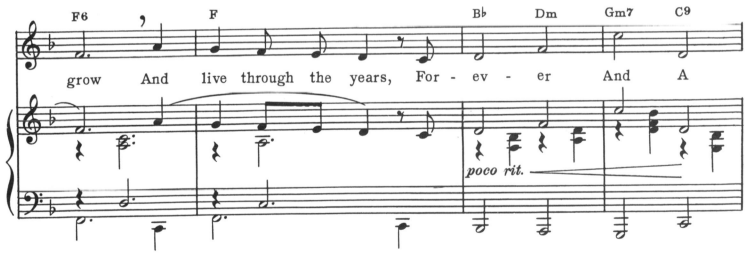

grow And live through the years, For - ev - er And A

poco rit.

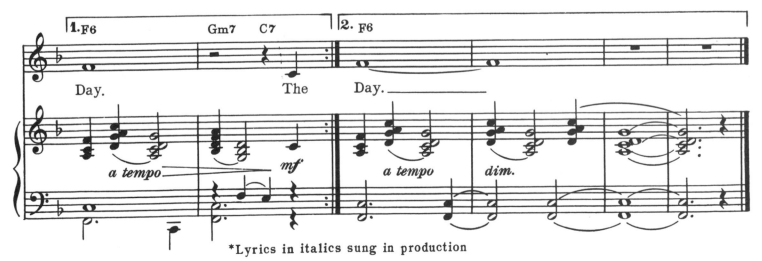

Day. The Day._____

a tempo *mf* *a tempo* *dim.*

*Lyrics in italics sung in production

from the Lester Osterman-Robert Fletcher-Richard Horner production "HIGH SPIRITS"

I KNOW YOUR HEART

Words and Music by HUGH MARTIN
and TIMOTHY GRAY

from the Lester Osterman-Robert Fletcher-Richard Horner production "HIGH SPIRITS"

YOU'D BETTER LOVE ME

Words and Music by HUGH MARTIN
and TIMOTHY GRAY

To - mor - row I ___ may fly ___ a - way. __

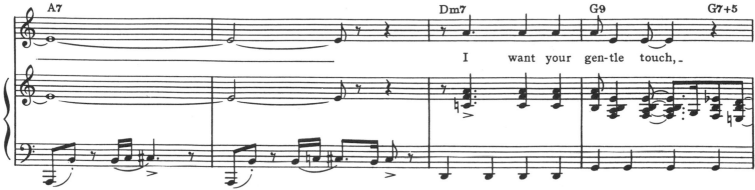

I want your gen - tle touch, __

Your con - ti - nen - tal touch, __ Your el - e - men - tal touch, __ And

you want me too, oh I know that you do. You'd Bet - ter Love __ Me while __ I'm here. __

I have __ been known __ to dis - ap - pear, __

So don't let this mir-a-cle__ melt a - way.__

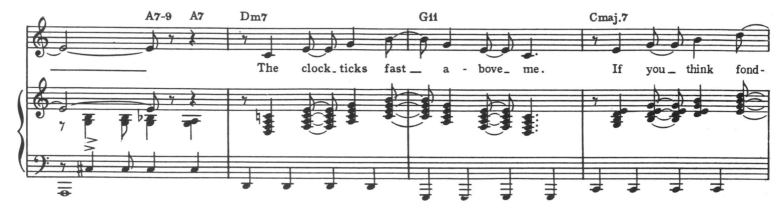

The clock__ ticks fast__ a - bove__ me. If you__ think fond-

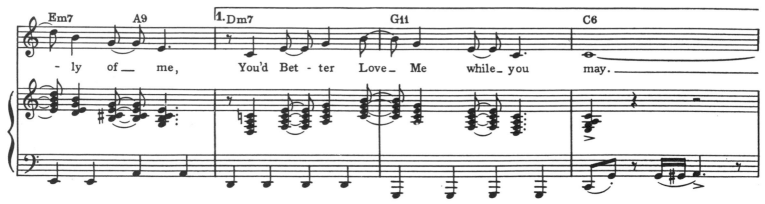

-ly of__ me, You'd Bet - ter Love__ Me while__ you may.__

You'd Bet - ter Love__ Me while you may.__

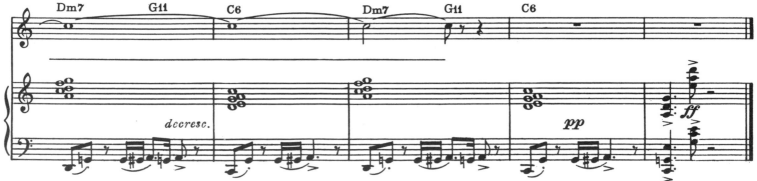